CW00522195

Southend Poetry 40 – 202

Southend Poetry Group, founded in the 1960s, ˅ ⸺ᵤ₉ₑₛ ᵤₑ reading, writing and appreciation of poetry. Membership is open to anyone who is interested in poetry.

Our meetings are on the first Monday of each month. We have a programme of talks about particular poets or poetic forms, presented by volunteer members, with some meetings for our own poems or workshops.

There is also a Facebook page where members can post poems and comments. New people have also joined in, becoming Facebook friends.

The Group has a policy of accepting submissions to the anthology from anyone who has attended two meetings during the year, or has posted on our Facebook page.

There are 20 poets published in this year's anthology, three are new members of the Group and one is from a Facebook friend.

© Copyright remains with the authors, 2024
ISBN No. 978-1-9163220-4-2

For further information visit our website:
www.southendpoetry.co.uk

or find us on Facebook listed as
Southend Poetry Group

For those not using the internet, Dorothy Turner, the Chair, can be reached on 01702 553191

Cover design and photography by Derek Adams

INDEX OF AUTHORS

Breakfast

A lonely breakfast in the small café
to the looping repetition
of a Presley croon

the isolation palpable
as Hopper's *Nighthawks*
or his *Morning Sun*

while separate tables echo
anonymity of hotel rooms
and mirror distance from each other -

morning strangers united
only in the shared experience
of solitude or loss

and mouthing the words
"I've found a new place to dwell
it's down at the end of lonely street"
with breakfast served at Heartbreak Hotel.

Adrian Green

From the River to the Sea

The dreams tossed over
London Bridge drift
slowly from the river
to the sea.

They pause at Thurrock's
tidal shore beside the ancient forts,
the post-industrial remains
of power station debris,

methane vents and broken glass
being ground to sand,
a beach of dreams
discarded in the mud.

Dredgers scour the riverbed,
carve out a channel
for the Gateway port downstream
where monsters berth

and the tide flows out past Canvey,
Southend and Montgomery wreck
until the Maunsell forts and windfarm
towers are left behind

and all the dreams absorbed
and nightmares exorcised
between the river and the sea.

Adrian Green

From the River to the Sea has appeared previously on the OU Poets'
website at https://oupoets.org.uk/editors-choice/

Time Boating

A journey up the *Smriti* River
Is not always an easy task
To re-live the exhilarating nausea
As the boat dives from crest to trough
While we row against the flow of time

Yesterday we were at the rock we remember
But that gap between the woods
Where we saw the flash of the momentary sun
Sprayed by the torrent in kaleidoscopic colours
Into our half averted eyes

Was that the day before or only a lifetime ago?

Bhaskar Dasgupta

Notes
Smriti: literally 'that which is remembered'; memories (Sanskrit)

Two Planets in my Sky

I don't know whence they came
What magic reaction of cosmic dust
What celestial music of the heavenly orbs
Attended their creation

They travelled the universe
On their chariot with three moons
The little boy was bemused by his galactic neighbours
He called to the passing asteroids, skipped along the Milky Way
Leaned out to touch the Red Dwarfs and Blue Giants
Lost his place and fell
Fell earthwards like Atlas' young daughter
Desperately clutching a shooting star

Vasundhara, the spouse of the sky
Picked up the little boy and gave him shelter, told him stories
Of what she had borne silently through the millennia
Of beauty and ugliness, of tears and joy
She showed him the mountains to climb, the seas to sail

He painted bisons and horses in the caves of Lascaux and Altamira
Hunted the lions with Assyrians in Babylon
Wrote on stone tablets with *Priyadarshin*, the Lion- Emperor
She taught him to read and write, to think and search.

One day she took him to the place where he fell from the sky
And taught him to Gaze

In the softness of a dark and stormy night
When the streetlights fade in the swirling haze
I listen to whispers from another world
I gaze into my sky and see them shining bright
I look at the Planets
They look back at me
Hold me tight
For an enduring instant eternity

Bhaskar Dasgupta

Notes
Vasundhara: name for mother earth (Sanskrit);
Priyadarshin: Pali name of the Indian monarch philosopher
Ashoka (BC 304-232) –'He who beholds everyone with affection'

Haiku

Pear by golden pear
Summer drips into Autumn
Each drop bears new life

Carol Ann Lintern

Mirror

What a poor portrait you paint.
Your sight is obscured by the dazzle of light
and is fooled by the camouflage of skin.
Your brush traces contours leaving unrevealed
the shallows and depths graven
into the face behind the face,
the face bearing trophies and scars,
eyes searching inwardly
and lips that mouth a silent song.

Carol Ann Lintern

Shops of happiness

I work in the workshop,
and sing in the sing shop,
and love in the love shop.

My arms around you,
your arms around me,
your breathing into mine,
and my soul into yours,
we'll dream in the dream shop.

Donatien Moisdon

HAIKU (Well, sort of…)

A ringing telephone.
Heart fluttering, I rush :
It wasn't you!

Donatien Moisdon

A Peaceful Life

All my life I've lived in peace,
though troops were returning
from Korea while Mum whirled
me on the park roundabout.

When newspaper headlines shouted
SUEZ, CYPRUS, MAU MAU
the only artillery I knew
was the soft explosion of snowballs
or the pop pop of cap pistols.

When I started work the news
was IRA bombs in London, Manchester
but my home town stayed untouched,
the soldiering was confined
to Northern Ireland.

Married, I took the children to the beach
to build sandcastles, collect shells.
Troops were fighting in Kuwait.
I used to cook roast dinners,
made mint sauce for the lamb
while warships sailed to the Falklands.

My children grew up and settled
in civilian jobs, never called-up
or trapped in besieged towns.
The wars went on elsewhere:
Iraq, or Afghanistan.

I spend my retirement in peace.
Commentators use the words 'battle lines'
to talk of politics. Here, we use
military language metaphorically.

Dorothy Turner

Different Kinds of Weather

From the porch we watched the storm
roll across the Canadian plain
for half an hour 'til we retreated to the warm

while a cloudburst lashed the window-pane
and lightning produced fantastic shows
I've never seen in England, nor will again.

A bitter U.S. winter, blizzard snows
remembered in Ted Kooser's poetry:
survivors; those lost in whiteness, who froze.

English hurricane leaves barely a tree
still standing, fells acres of forest,
garden favourites. Root-plates attract the mason bee.

A plume of sand on the wind, where will it rest?
Captured on a Met Office satellite shot
it's heading towards Europe, north, north west.

Global systems, interlinked, weather's not
so easy to control - we accept our lot.

Dorothy Turner

Little Bird

a sonnet for Janet, my Galah

I have a book they say is true,
and so it is, my dear, but still it is not you.
I read your poem of the awfulness of love;
you are 'my little bird' whose heartfelt words I have.

How, by some irony of distance, we are friends
I do not know. I turn to other thoughts instead:
mostly, I think there is a keenness distance lends.
I still remember that first poem of yours I read …

Fair go, Galah, over the Sydney Harbour Bridge.
Fair go, Galah, under the shade of eucalypts.
Fair go, Galah. Perhaps we'll meet beyond the edge?
Perhaps we'll walk together, after *my* eclipse?

I've never sat with you to tell you, heart to heart.
How much of life I've wasted, waiting for the start.

Evelyn Grace Quinlan

Croppe Ridig

after a painting by Angela Deary

Love is most nearly itself
When here and now cease to matter
T. S. Eliot - Four Quartets: East Coker

Time past has ceased to pass:
this is the story of the water.
Our love is like a looking-glass
in which we do not see the future
—all that falls, what will not last—
only the here and now that matter.

This is the teaching of the stone,
which knows the lesson of the lichen:
the stillness of the buried bone;
the blood that will no longer quicken;
the lover who is long since gone;
the children who will one day sicken;
how love, at length, is overgrown;
how every lover is twice smitten.

Only reflect on *being* still;
picture the bloom not going over.
So much alive, with time to kill ...
This day will do, for this day's lover:
this sun and air, this glorious hill,
this sky, these clouds, this simple river.

Evelyn Grace Quinlan

The Reader

My eyes chased the candlelight in a darkened room,
The stylus hummed over each melodic groove,
An open fire disturbed, hissed, crackled and nudged
The stubborn ember, that shifted out of sight.
I focused my gaze, and caught her gentle smile,
Deep in thought, her senses raised at each turn of the page,
Caressing each leaf softly with trembling fingertips
As the words danced in the reflection of her
Deep brown eyes, aflame with a burning desire.

Every word spirited her away into the realm of
Dreams in the embrace of that old armchair.
It never complained, but wrapped itself around her,
Comforting, embracing, touching and holding her gently
In its arms, as she journeyed in time to unknown lands,
The headrest peering over her well-formed shoulders
Like the benevolent spirit of a curious guardian.

The fire crackled and spat with envy,
The flames just shadow danced.
Her every move slow, purposeful,
Snuggling deeper into her lover's arms,
Her silken gown fought to maintain
Her modesty and discreetly covered
Her velvet ebony skin, whilst
The candles flickered with excitement.

As the new dawn bursts into colour to light up an idyllic sky,
With a heavy heart and a sigh, she turned the final page,
Her eyelids beckoning her to sleep.
She smiled at me, that secret smile that lover's share,
And as she stirred, her hair caressed the nape of her slender neck
And gently brushed against her cheek adorned with light,
Like the final brushstroke to a treasured masterpiece,
And she slowly drifted off to sleep, in the comfort
Of the old armchair, to the echoes of Hiawatha's Wedding Feast

Michelle Smith

Breathe

You touch my heart
Although I hesitate

You stir my soul
It wants to sing

I search your eyes
They speak your inner truth

I hold my breath
And feel your gentle touch

I grasp at hope
And feel a trembling heart

You are my peace
You give me wings

Michelle Smith

The Low Winter Sun

In the heart of winter's icy grip
I embark on a journey dodging cosmic tricks
A blazing, mischievous fire ball playing games
A dazzling blinding journey through the dancing rays

Low in the sky an intense radiant orb burns
Distracting blinding disorientating my eyes hurt
In the glare the ribbon of grey shining like a mirror
In the chaos all lanes, markings pavements disappear

With my palm I shield, I squint, I pull down the shades
Like bullies they creep through the windshield
the daring rays
When the symphony of light flares at a blinding pace

A relentless glare, for a driver a challenging quest
Driving on, in defiance in this solar ballet,
When the low winter sun shines
it's a juggling cosmic tango along the way

Irie Perera

The Music Room

In the heart of the house there was a vibrant room
Where youngsters played, where melodies bloomed
The first stumbling scales, sipping arpeggios and chords
The first trials at the brass sounded like mooing of the cows
Through frustrations and tears they held there with passion
The adolescent and the music room a haven of cheer
The faint echoes of melodies linger in the air
The children now adults spreading their wings elsewhere

Where once a boy played violin's first creaky shrieks
'Vivaldi's Four Seasons' a symphony dancing on strings
A piano sits in solitude, no more Beethoven's streams
We long for those gifted hands the ivories scream
They blew their lungs off, for the passion of jazz
Now they've left home, the muted silence, the deep despair
Oh! how the room yearns for the notes with the old flare.

Irie Perera

His Choice

A man cherishes a dream sincere.
That everybody living in Russia
Can express an opinion, without fear.
His wife he knew he would not be able to see

For his beliefs, he was arrested and put on trial.
The State decided to classify him as a criminal.
Isolation from public support was now assured.
In prison he would be locked up like an animal.

Alexie Navalny is the name to be remembered.
He fell ill soon after the start of his sentence.
In hospital he should have died from poisoning.
The poison was intended to end his existence.

From hospital he was smuggled out and escaped.
In Germany the medics nursed Alexie back to health.
Novichok was the poison intended to kill him.
The decision not to stay in exile he made himself.

His choice was to stay in Germany and remain safe,
Or return to Russia exposing the damning state crime
Of intended murder to the world and publicise the fact.
To return to Russia took even more courage this time.

He was arrested again as soon as the plane landed
A breach of parole to save his life was the charge.
Twelve and a half years was the sentence for this absence.
A prison in Siberia ensured contact to be extremely scarce.

While he lived the world was watching.

Colin Riley

He plays the guitar

The sweet sound of music
Caresses that drum in your ear.
Your foot start tapping with the rhythm
Then your whole body shakes with vibration.

The style he plays is called the blues
Blues that make you feel happy, but not sad.
Its origins are in the cotton fields in Mississippi;
To make you feel and think of happier times.

These musicians have long, long gone before
Big Bill Broonzy, Reverend Gary Davis, Mississippi John Hurt,
To name just a few; that brought entertainment to you,
In addition, the contentment and ecstasy that feeds your very
 soul.

The melody and the rhythm, he plays simultaneously
In a finger style technique. A gift for all to admire.
He was not born in the deep South, as you might think but
Strangely enough in East London, in Canning Town E16.

Colin Riley

Indian Roads

Endless
Clinging to contours like drowning sailors
Strings of villages
Dogs dozing s
A rhythm of shops
Where no-one seems to buy
Festooned with streamers of ancient western crisps
And cubes of sweets
Sweating in glass cabinets.
Herds of motorbikes
Gather by a grimy workshop
Where no-one seems to work
And a lone cow owns the road.
All let him pass
Like a mad king.

Ceaseless spirals
Steep green ravines,
Where vast villas, obnoxiously new
Sprout like weeds
And – at every stopping place
Huge garish teddies
Cheap pink-skinned dolls
Jostle with brass curry cauldrons
Aluminium ladles
And tasselled rugs in muted tones.
Miles below
A river
Rippling since the beginning of time.

A woman walks the road
Logs on her shoulder
A pot on her head
Slow, sedate, graceful as a queen.
A lorry shimmies past, flaunting silver strips
Its sides tell a rainbow story
Its horn sings a symphony.
Tortuous twists
Wooden carts offer a wealth of vegetables
Ruby carrots,
Golden moon bananas,
And cauliflower pearls
Nestling in emerald shells
A girl sits immobile on a mat,
Her pyramid of apples
Glow in the reflection of her scarlet sari.
And always a random café
Men assemble to right their world
On circles of plastic chairs
Miraculously morphed from English tips
To land here
On dusty roadsides
While women
Labour unseen.

Indian roads
Endless
Blessed by the sun.

Sue Lesser

According to HIS - torians
(Pandora's Lament)

They say the king of the gods commanded it
And a lesser god created me.
I was a plot to punish Prometheus
(as if his chains were not enough!)
Thus man made woman in retribution.
But I say not so!
For I have always been here:
Earth-mother, Gaia, Pachamama,
On my wheel of life
I threw the very world where these boy-gods played,
Fired it in the sun's kiln,
Hung it in the heavens.

They say I was weak,
Unable to master temptations,
Crippled by curiosity,
Disobedient as Eve.
But I say not so!
For I was bold to challenge the divine edict,
Dare to defy the omnipotent,
Strong to standup for my rights.

They say I released all evil to the world.
But I say not so!
For surely it was already here,
In male deities who disobeyed, judged and sentenced.
And seeking an excuse to explain, happened on woman!

And so it has always been – we bear the blame for their
transgressions,
We are the mothers failing sinful sons, the rape victims who
asked for it,
The dead who deserved it.

They say I bestowed hope
I say yes, I'll take that.

Sue Lesser

The Poet's Art

A poet is a poor man's minstrel;
A wordsmith without a musical instrument.
He has a voice, but he can't sing,
And yet he has the wherewithal to bring
A bit of sunshine into our life
And create some meaning out of strife,
To make some sense of a disturbing world
And create some beauty when his words are unfurled.
He can put into words what we feel in our heart,
And paint pictures in our mind - that's the poet's art...

Malcolm Wright

Sparrows

Out of all our feathered friends,
Sparrows are the last you'd commend.
They're not much loved by anyone.
Their plain-clothed outfits not much fun.
They flit from bush to bush;
Always in such a rush...
Ducking and diving, catching flies,
Making more noise than befits their small size.
They squeak and squabble all day long,
But we'd miss them if they were gone...

Malcolm Wright

Boot Sale at Leigh

Rows of open cars inviting,
darkness is soon lifting
to the dawn of a Sunday.
Gravel underfoot, dirty, dusty
selling goods profitably
scuffed records ragged books
for discerning folk; literature
a windswept fluttering of hanging garments
never on a rainy day though.
Worship the bargain found and given
with dealers on site rapidly
no taxation to their conscience
they crowd in the new arrivals.

Yesterday's gadgets, playthings
even cheap tinned food
and faded time pieces pass.
Find, barter to collect
think of beating the system
before midday
then the feast of beef commences.
Burning of burgers as a prelude
occasional airborne cigarette smoke
rings adorn those grasping fingers
as leathered men scan for:
The Beatles.

Warren Farley

To Have Or To Be

Be done with fads and trends
violently rejecting social media
you were once a slave within it
and nobody knew who you were
least of all your very self
because they were all one the same
as is everyone else.

Now go quietly amongst the noise and haste
be polite, caring, humble.
Be in the world yet no part of it
evolve from your flaws, seek healing
serve no grasping master
compete with nobody, because you're wiser.

Sleep long and deep by night
from darkness search the inner light, learn
rely on no one for your happiness
value friendship before romance
be not quite so lustful as the others.

Laugh at governments, nuisance as they are,
stumbling from each tyranny to the next
to Hell with mortgages and nice cars
know not chaos and screaming
govern yourself, be someone
more remarkable in fact

turning negative to positive
avoiding those who would judge you
as they bloody will, jealously.
Be not ashamed
to scorn their material wealth
they are not well
and you are purest gold.

We are the gods if we but knew it
and reality leaves us largely alone …
I could kill with my kindness.

Warren Farley

One Day in Smithfield

The magistrate has spoken.
A trial of sorts was heard.
A spell must now be broken
To restore the sacred word.

No evidence presented,
Just the stated grudge,
The common sense of people
When a bias will not budge.

Out the dirty gates of Newgate
A wagon weighed with witch
Hobbles over cobbles,
Painful in its pitch.

And amidst the horrid curses
And the slander to be slung,
The rotting veg confetti
Of excrement and dung,

It makes its way to Smithfield
Where driftwood pyres await,
Where a loud bloodthirsty throng
Await their lust be sate.

A match will catch the kindle,
Flames will find her feet.
Screams will scratch the silence.
Flesh will turn to meat.

Some regret the fervour,
Haunted by her dying breath.
Some will check their morals,
But more will relish death.

And in the end the crowd disperse
To justify their thirst,
For the anguish of another
In a world that does its worst.

Phil Swain

The End of Life Benches

Approaching a favourite place,
I sense something is amiss,
but don't know what.

I do a double take:
there is the lawn terrace,
a recess, off the seafront;
there the attractive fringe
of shrubs and evergreens;
there is the walkway;
there the line of benches,
each with its memorial plaque
But this is now, I know,
a kind of Death Row:
a line of the condemned,
benches beyond care and attention,
notified "End of Life".

Then I realise,
with some shock,
one has already been -
despatched:
the book-end bench,
my favourite one,

Of course all the while,
the ageing had been going on:
the timbers turning pallid grey,
the wood splintering,
then cracking;
now some of the seating slats
are bent and broken;
and hang down,
loose and limp,
in gestures of death.

I stand and stare:
after some while,
I walk along the line,
take an accustomed seat,
and look out across
The estuary reach.

Weeks later, none are there,
and where I used to sit and muse,
The terrace walk is bare.

John Hennebry

Icarus

A gallery sculpture,
in sea-green bronze,
arrested me:
Icarus, escaping;
arms outstretched,
chest bare, face gaunt,
expression anguished,
the bees wax melting,
his wing ragged.

It brought to mind a friend,
soaring,
at the peak of his mania,
exultant with hubris,
exhilarated with his own certainty -
oblivious to danger.

But then his Fall:
mid sentence,
with his arm pointing,
flamboyantly towards the sky,
dropping to the ground,
in sudden seizure,
like a sack of spuds
off the back of a lorry.

And then,
for months afterwards,
night after night,
saturated in his sleep,
drowning in his own urine.

John Hennebry

Dividers

Nasty geometry things, dividers
compasses with points on both legs.
Malicious cads poke others with them.

But the big dividers are worse
giving whole populations
urges to poke at others.

Race is one, applied widely,
language another;
misogyny sure enough divides

And places, hills and valleys,
borders, rivers and seas, fences,
hedges of varying depths and heights;

Aspects of culture, choices
food, dress, behavioural norms
all dividers for prodding,

Poking verbally, crass jokes,
belittling jibes, derogatory memes,
vainglorious songs and slogans.

And to crown it all
in the guise of goodness
comes a super divider, religion.

But let's be fair;
its more sincere practitioners
are against poking.

Denis Ahern

Romantic Verse?

I can list the ingredients,
All that stuff on valentine cards,
Fragrant blossoms, luxury chocs,
Endearing guff, pink ribbon in yards,

Moonlight, summer breeze, flattery,
Lies that seem to come from the heart,
I know that's the stuff that's needed.
Versifying it all's the hard part.

I'm rubbish at romantic verse
I'm just too much of a cynic.
If my love was like a red, red rose
I'd get myself to a clinic.

Denis Ahern

This vulnerability

this strength

this parthenogenic
Mystery

that is the human v divine polarity

This Malignant political
Double indemnity

both cause and effect,
Simultaneously

The very paradox
of a human condition
mirrored & mirroring
Consubstantiality

giving rise to a
contrapuntal argument
eternally consequent.

Each 'I' began when
Woman and Man conceived
a plan
to have and hold
and then remould
Human identity

Isobel Grindley

You'll be lucky

If you can get to thirty without any debt,
if you get past your twenties with no grey hairs set,
if you can speak another language and use it well,
if you can only really tell people
what it is today they should sell,
if you get the chance to see a deer in the wild,
or even just manage to have room to sit down
for a while,
if you can ever match the socks together
in your drawers,
After 7 pints with the lads still read off the TV
"what are the scores?"

> If you ever got the
> pleasure of being thanked for your time
> be in that moment to do everything you can
> to make an experience sublime,
> even if it's a light
> when the stressed need to smoke,
> a friend needs a shoulder to make wet as,
> with heavy hands their head they cloak.
> You'll be lucky,

Breaking bread with those who even need it emotionally,
taking pleasure in the selfless,
that's never truly selfless; destruction of the very meaning
when you feel so high of the surprise help gives,
you'll touch the ceiling.
A burning, white hot full on gun shot of energy,
yearning for the time you can do more,
tally them up dude, keep yourself a score,
happiness is all that matters now,
with deadly disease
your memories can be robbed
and leave you wondering; How?

You'll be lucky and love it
keep it close and cherish the hit,
it becomes a drug of enveloping warm hugs
as the bad energy you shrug away makes the day a better
place to stay.

As much as they will be,
you my friend, will be lucky.

R.J. Learmouth

Life on Teams

A window into someone else's world -
connections are fragmented
boredom is aligned.
The same questions,
The same answers -
get to the point!
I am wasting precious minutes.
I am bored.
I could be more useful in that time
and also, I need my tea fix.

Maria Jones

The Commute

A squirrel on the track!
Mind yourself Mr Squirrel!
The lovely yellow and orange of the morning sky,
a lovely sight that morning.
The wood cutter's workshop -
a memorial,
a tribute to my father.
When I see the train
he is in my mind's eye.

Maria Jones

Poems of colour are a black and white issue?

Pre '69
In the darkness before colour tv,
we watched filthy apartheid happening abroad,
and at home, the Black and White Minstrels.
During the best of these times,
sunshine beamed-in greyscale
through Lennon's *kaleidoscope skies.*
So much so, back then,
you'd have been forced to read
the dulled-edged words of this poem
in monochromed celluloid,
held up against the light,
frame by shadowed frame.

Post '70
Gill Scott-Heron preached,
"The Revolution Will Not Be Televised".
Though later, binary divisions caused
feral spy cameras and video screens to replicate,
covering walls and watchtowers like ivy,
filming everything, rolling news 24/7.
In truth, few staring down deep into their phones
would become angered enough
to *plug in, turn on and cop out*;
and let's be honest with ourselves,
riots of colour-bursting text,
a call-to-arms underscored
by psychedelic paisley grooves,
aren't going to bellow by themselves.

Today
The 'Roaring Twenties' whimper on.
Often silenced on mute,
no yawp or rebel yell,
only an ocean of pastoral watercolours
drowning the King's English,
or slightly better still,
our *Republican Estuary* English.
But keep watching spectrums on the horizon
and listening out for the shout;
for those choking charcoal clouds above us
are gathering apace,
whilst the wider world goes on make-believing
a far brighter place.

Phil East

All that Glistens

I once wrote a love poem,
Not too long,
not too short.
And when presenting it,
I said it was priceless
yet worth its weight in gold
- but to keep it all the same,
since it might appreciate over time.

Paper is worthless,
it carries no weight,
so I'd delicately scalpelled off
the words, the letters, the punctuation,
and laid the fragments of veneer
each wafer-thin as gold leaf
in a ring box, itself
satin-lined and gilt-edged.

To keep safe from damage
and away from the light,
it was then flat-packed in cardboard
and the package labelled:
'FRAGILE - POEM – HANDLE WITH CARE".
The poem came complete
with its own self-assembly instructions
plus an alan key (as a joke).

Years later,
I heard she'd sold up
and moved away.
I imagine she'd cashed in:
taking the poem to Cashconverters.
After all, I'd said
it was priceless
and worth its weight in gold.

I imagined the pawnshop man saying,
"*The bottom has dropped out*
of the vintage verse market"
- but placing it on the scales nonetheless,
gram for gram of gold,
he agreed to pay over an old silver sixpence
for the sentimental value,
it being better than nothing.   ***Phil East***

Jamaican Lady

This Jamaican lady has her own style.
She greets people with her infectious smile.

Her wild hairstyle is red, yellow and green.
She's been creative since she was a teen.

She loves to watch waterfalls and mountains.
She likes to cook rice and peas with plantains.

She often travels around Jamaica;
Where she likes to bring tourists together.

She walks barefoot on the soft sandy beach;
Eating mangoes and a sweet juicy peach.

She can walk for miles in the countryside;
And will often take a bicycle ride.

She goes to parties where she loves dancing;
With her friends who think she is a blessing.

They drink Bob Marley cocktails at the bar;
This is a tribute to the reggae star.

She dances with men who are romantic;
To the sounds of caribbean music.

She is laid-back, hospitable and nice.
She lives life to the full; in paradise.

Paulette Green

written from the painting: Jamaican Lady – 2023
by Paulette Green

We want Love and Peace

War and hatred is not the solution.
Why do innocent lives have to perish?
We want love and peace for the whole nation.

Stop the violence; come to a conclusion;
This is not the time to be cruel and selfish.
War and hatred is not the solution.

Think of the future; show some compassion,
Give people a chance to shine and flourish.
We want love and peace for the whole nation.

Make this a happy New Year's resolution;
And bring colour to our dreams; to embellish.
War and hatred is not the solution.

Let's pray for hope, in times of confusion;
And hope things will get better; that is my wish.
We want love and peace for the whole nation.

We want the best for the next generation,
So they can look back on good times, to cherish.
War and hatred is not the solution;
We want love and peace for the whole nation.

Paulette Green

Notes on Contributors

Denis Ahern – Cork born, Essex based, carpenter, fire-fighter, weight-lifter, musician, comedian, poet who counts his failures on his fingers, his successes on his thumbs, opts for shallow and accessible over deep and obscure

Bhaskar Dasgupta's love for poetry and passion for Indian classical music is inspired by the twin Bards of Bengal Rabindranath Tagore and Nazrul Islam. He has written and staged many shows in London including the musical Kavita K2K (Indian poetry from Kalidas to Kaifi Azmi) written entirely in English verse, He maintains his musical and poetry interests alongside an internationally renowned career as a clinician and researcher.

Phil East If poetic subject matter were divvied-up, Phil would lay claim to cannibalism; Sputnik; stoned fruit; darker shades of the colour blue; vultures; hypocrisy in high places; dance crazes; sand varying in size from a single grain to a beach-full; and the stretch of estuary between Benfleet Creek and Southend Pier.

Adrian Green has published 3 full collections, *Chorus and Coda* (2007), *All That Jazz and Other Poems* (2018) and *New Blues and Other Poems* (2023), all from The Littoral Press. His work has appeared in magazines and anthologies in England and abroad, and in every issue of Southend poetry since 1985

Paulette Green's autobiography is on hold until the near future. She is planning a new self-published book of more villanelles and haikus.

Isobel Grindley BA (Hons) grew up in Southend worked as a Care Assistant and most enjoyed hosting student visitors and teaching English to speakers of other languages (TESOL).

John Hennebry – A teacher of English for 30 odd years. Semi-retired – mercifully! Aims to write more poetry now.

Maria Jones lives in Southend on Sea and is a Civil Servant. This is Maria's first submission to the anthology and is looking forward to contributing more in the future.

RJ Learmouth is a non-binary poet and artist from Southend. The poem 'You'll be Lucky' which can be found in their debut book 'Meretricious' focuses on an inward analysis of what it is to be lucky in a modern society, making light of trivial things and highlighting elements of selflessness.

Sue Lesser - a poet who loves reading and writing poetry and performing at local open-mic events. She has published 2 volumes of poetry and used them to raise money for dementia charities, also four novels and a collection of short stories. All her books are available on Amazon.

Carol Ann Lintern - made a chance visit to the Southend Poetry Group and, to her surprise, found that poetry was what she had been looking for.

Donatien Moisdon started as an air traffic controller (control tower in an airport) then went on to become a teacher of French and English. He has had several novels published in French, including one that was short-listed for Prix Fémina. In English, his short story *Animals* won first prize in a Radio Kent short story competition and broadcast twice on Radio 4. He has two novels on Amazon: *School of Contempt* in paperback and *Bestial* as an e-book.
Your own literary reviews would be more than welcome. Thank you.

Irie Perera joined the poetry group in 2019. 'I have really enjoyed writing poems during the lockdown which kept me occupied and got me thinking. I like to write about good and bad life experiences of people'.

Evelyn Quinlan was born much later than you'd imagine, and fortunately, therefore, her juvenilia went unwritten. Her senilia, however, is in full flood. She previously published widely under a *nom de plume* (Philip Quinlan), but is now flying solo, wearing different feathers, and loving it. Hurrah for samsara! (S)he previously co-edited Angle Journal of Poetry in English, though said journal has sadly now departed to that bourne from which none returns.

Colin Riley - was born in Epping Forest. He became interested in poetry after he retired from work. He sometimes finds innovation in writing about inspirational people or interesting events. He also enjoys reading other peoples' poems.

Michelle Smith left London in 2001 and moved to Leigh on Sea, which has been a source of inspiration. Her poems have appeared in several editions of the Southend Poetry Anthology.

Dorothy Turner has always liked reading poetry and started writing seriously in the 1990s. Joined the Southend Poetry Group in 1996 and is now Chairman. Recently published her first poetry collection 'About Time and Other Poems'.

Malcolm Wright was a regular at Southend Poetry Group in its early years and some of his poems appeared in earlier anthologies. He has also had poems published in The Lady, People's Friend, This England and Amateur Gardening, as well as in numerous little magazines.